ABiGAiL's AMAZiNG DAD

Dedicated to Wilson E. Maines

Be on the lookout for the hidden butterflies as you turn each page.

Butterflies symbolize love and angels. I think of my dad every time I see a butterfly.

Do you want your daughter to write a book about you someday?

Yes? Then this book is for YOU.

Ever since I can remember, I have been blessed with a deep inner confidence that allows me to be courageous, competitive, direct, honest, resilient, focused, confident, and fierce.

I have been called all of these things since my earliest days. I never feel self-conscious about these terms.
Rather, I am proud.

I am proud and loved telling my dad about my school and later, career experiences with these adjectives. He was never surprised.

See, I am a "Maines Girl."

I was reared to be exactly who I am. My dad never doubted me for a second. I knew that.

From the day I was born, he made me feel like the most important, smartest, and kindest person in the world.

I have spent the last four-plus decades reflecting on how he empowered me. What exactly did he do? I wanted to reflect and understand him so I can share with dads and moms and really anyone who wants to dramatically improve someone's self-esteem and their life overall.

That brings me to this story. This book is based on my early years with my dad, my elementary school years to be specific. I clearly remember that formative time and have found myself reflecting on it since my early twenties.

The characters could be updated to fit the current decade, but that I leave up to you, the reader.

Who would you replace Ann and Margaret with?

"Abigail!"

"What, Dad?" Abigail yelled from her bedroom.

"Come downstairs, hurry!" exclaimed her dad.

Abigail sighed, dropped her journal, and hurried downstairs.

"What is it, Dad?"

Her dad turned to her with a huge smile and said,
"Sit down and listen to this.

Treasurer Ann Richards is an absolute dynamo."

Abigail's Dad was clearly smitten with the Treasurer of Texas, Ms. Ann Richards.

As Abigail sat down to listen, she couldn't help but get excited. Ann was full of energy, intelligence, charm, and heart.

The TV came alive when she was speaking.

"If you give women a chance, we can perform. After all, Ginger Rogers did everything Fred Astair did. She just did it backwards and in high heels."

Her dad hung on every word.

Abigail could tell he was fired up by Ann just like the live audience who were hooting and hollering on the TV.

"Abigail, Ann should be in charge of everything! Don't you think? She makes this look easy."

Abigail pleaded with her dad for sassy boots so she could "be like Ann."

"Dad, I had a dream about Ann last night.

She told me to run for Governor of New York.

Isn't that crazy?

She told me New York needs a girl like me!"

Abigail's Dad looked at her
with kind eyes and said,

"You can be President.

**You can be anything
you want.**

I can't wait to see all the
amazing things you will do, and
you will change the world.
Just like Ann."

Abigail headed off to school full of excitement to share stories about Ann with her friends.

She told Jennifer and Chantelle all about Ann's big hair and how everyone in the audience hung on her every word.

"I think Ann is my dad's hero!" Abigail exclaimed.

The three girls talked about what speeches they would give when they grew up.

Jennifer said, "I would talk about how to take care of animals."

Chantelle said, "I want to tell everyone how to play softball."

"I'd tell everyone all about my dad," said Abigail.

The next weekend it happened again!

"ABIGAIL, hurry!" her dad yelled from the living room.

Her dad had the same big smile and was obviously impressed with the woman on the TV with the British accent.

"Abigail, you have to hear Margaret. I am learning so much. She is fierce, determined, and unapologetic.

Isn't she great?"

Abigail couldn't disagree and, although she had no idea who Margaret was, she understood her dad's reaction to this confident and charismatic woman making her TV come alive just like Ann.

"If you want something said, ask a man. If you want something done, ask a woman."

Later that day, Abigail heard her dad telling his friend,
"Margaret may be controversial, but she is brave and
willing to say what she means.

You don't see that very often in today's politics."

As Abigail grew, she began to notice a pattern.

Her dad respected strong women. She saw it every day with his mom, Abigail's grandmother, his wife, Abigail's mom, and his youngest daughter, Sophia, too.

They were always celebrated, prioritized, and loved unconditionally.

Abigail saw firsthand what that support meant to the women in her family. They thrived, both personally and professionally. Their confidence was high.

Their energy was replenished after spending time with her dad.

Ann also thrived, becoming the Governor of Texas three years after Abigail first heard her speak with her dad in their living room.

YES!

WE ♥ ANN

GO ANN! 100%

ANN IS #1

"I have very strong feelings about how you lead your life...

You always look ahead. You never look back."

ANN'S PATH TO GOVERNOR

"You can do anything!"

"You are never afraid to ask questions!"

As Abigail grew, she loved to learn.

She found teachers who, like her dad, believed she could be anything. They did everything they could to help her reach her goals.

"We stand on the cusp of greatness!"

"I'm proud of you, Abigail!"

Abigail was a high achiever in school.

She was very focused and competitive academically.
She graduated at the top of her class.

Abigail, don't let anything slow you down,
you won't remember it in ten years.

Her Dad celebrated every milestone.

He was her biggest cheerleader when she played soccer and ran for class president.

Abigail always played the best when he was in the stands.

Even on bad days, he was in her corner.

He hyped her up when she was down.

Abigail's dad was the first person she called to celebrate and to cry. He always knew the right thing to say.

Abigail began her career in the business world.

She enjoyed work and the people she worked with.

She quickly learned that not all men are like her dad and not all women had developed the self- confidence that she had as a young girl.

At her first company, a male colleague said,

"This girl is trying to change everything."

Abigail knew that was not a compliment.

But you know what? She just didn't care.

She remembered Ann's bravery.

She remembered Margaret's confidence and resolve.

Those memories gave her strength to ignore the
voices she heard around her.

Today, Abigail continues to celebrate women like
her dad would want.

She is inspired by the strength of "Everyday Superheroes"
like teachers, nurses, and all women
who are using their voice and energy to help make
our world better.

Ann Richards

Margaret Thatcher

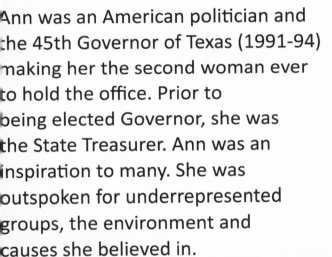

Ann was an American politician and the 45th Governor of Texas (1991-94) making her the second woman ever to hold the office. Prior to being elected Governor, she was the State Treasurer. Ann was an inspiration to many. She was outspoken for underrepresented groups, the environment and causes she believed in.

Margaret was a British politician and stateswoman who served as the first female Prime Minister of the United Kingdom from 1979 to 1990. She also holds the record for the longest serving Prime Minister. Margaret was known for her bravery.

Connect with us!

Web: fiercenow.org Instagram: @fierce_now LinkedIn: @fiercenow.org

FIERCE: Females In Every Role Change Everything.

FIERCE is grounded in an unwavering focus on empathy, resilience, and courage. Our mission is to accelerate the success of woman and girls in business, government, and academia for the betterment of themselves, their families, their communities, and the world.

FIERCE

Worksheet

Completed by someone who loves me.

_____ , you are so _____ and _____ .

I am proud of you when you _____ and _____ .

When you are _____ you remind me of _____ .

When you _____ it makes me think about _____ .

As you get older, I enjoy watching you _____ .

I hope you know how _____ I think you are every day.

I tell everyone you are _____ and _____ .

SIGNATURE _____ DATE _____

Download free copies of this worksheet at www.FierceNow.org

CPSIA information can be obtained
at www.ICGtesting.com
Printed in the USA
LVHW010820180523
747144LV00028B/597

9 781953 978172